Intermediate Studies

for

Developing Artists

on the Trumpet

by

Howard Hilliard

Published by
Meredith Music Publications
a division of G.W. Music, Inc.
1584 Estuary Trail, Delray Beach, Florida 33483
http://www.meredithmusic.com

Cover Photo: © 2009 Goktug Gurellier / istockphoto
Cover Design: Shawn Girsberger

International Standard Book Number: 978-1-57463-223-1
Printed and bound in U.S.A.

Introduction

Many famous musicians have been quoted saying, there are only two kinds of music: good and bad. I've done my best to find good music that covers every possible style appropriate to an intermediate book for brass. Taken together, Vol. 1 and 2 comprise a tour through Western music starting with a treatment of the fifteenth century melody "La Folia" up to the beginning of the twentieth century from dozens of countries, including my own compositions that mimic many historic styles. The musical selections outside the standard repertoire compare well in quality to the more famous works and have unique elements in them that increase the musical vocabulary of the student.

In addition to the classical etudes, both the trumpet and trombone editions have a significant number of jazz etudes written in a more formalized style that accurately represent most of the important jazz styles including: Dixieland, Swing, Bebop, Blues, and various Latin forms. Compositions by Bruce Wermuth and Chris Seiter raised the bar for my own jazz etudes. Their flexibility in working with me helped to achieve what I believe is a unique contribution to the jazz etude genre.

Special thanks to Michael Cichowicz and Balquhidder Music for permission to use an adapted portion of the flow study warm-up from *Long Tone Studies* by Vincent Cichowicz. There are a small number of targeted exercises that support specific etudes. Particular attention has been paid to achieve a balance of keys in the book. The specialized scales at the back of the book prepare the student for the keys covered in the book while also adding additional pedagogical elements.

With the advent of braces, many of the older method books are not feasible because of the high range. Particular attention has been made to give the student with braces gratifying and challenging music in a comfortable range. The goal of using good music is to entice as many students as possible into the beauty of making great music and to make practicing feel as effortless and as enriching as possible. A secondary byproduct of this book is to give the teacher something, with which to teach phrasing and, to escape the monotony of hearing the same mundane exercises over and over.

It is my sincere hope that both teacher and student will find the materials in this collection inspiring to play and artistically rewarding.

Howard Hilliard

4

Menuet

French
early 18th c.

French Dance

19th c.

Dance of the Pharaohs

French
early 18th c.

King of Sweden's March

19th c.

Water Music

Suite I

Händel

Royal Wedding Dance

19th c.

Flow Study

Cichowicz

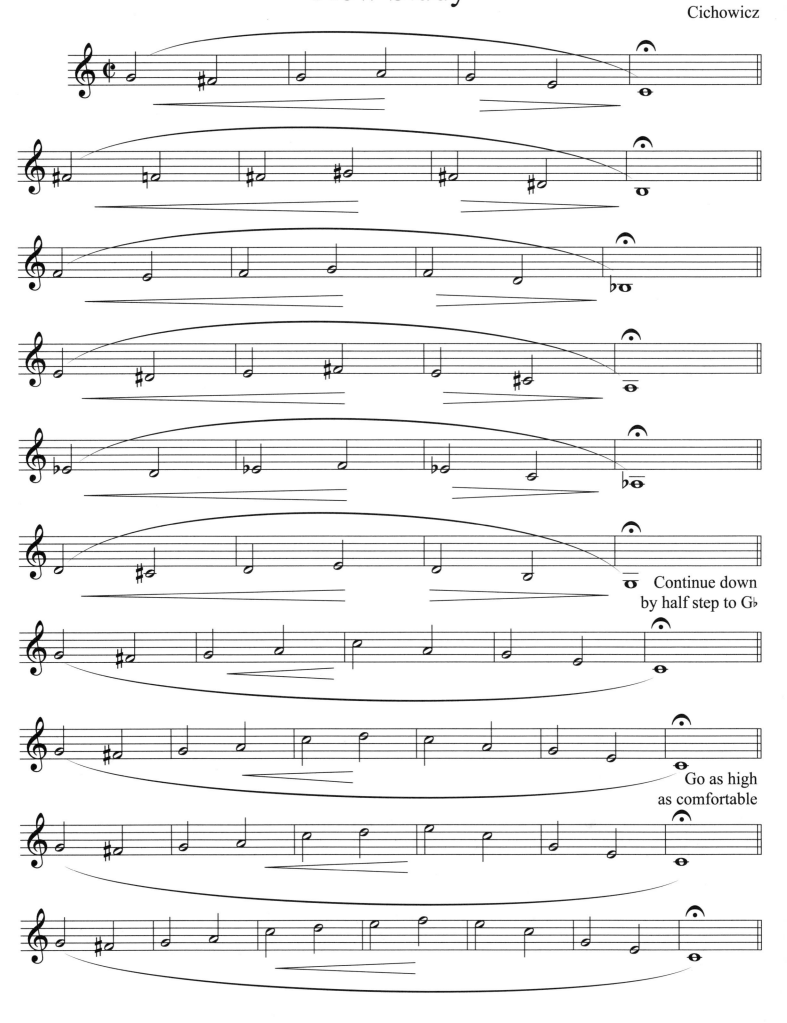

Continue down
by half step to G♭

Go as high
as comfortable

Direction

Hilliard

Arban

Hooked by Degree

Hilliard

Kling

Adagio Espressivo

p

cresc.

f

rit.

Jig

Hilliard

Minuet

Hilliard

mf

Chromatic

Hilliard

Arban

Pie Jesu

Fauré

Rudolf

Hilliard

Triumphal March

from the opera "Aida"

Verdi

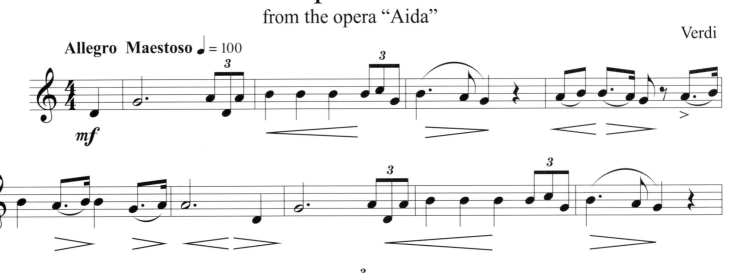

Exuberance

Hilliard

Gavotta

Corelli

Hilliard

Lip Slur

Hilliard

Mambo Slurs

Hilliard

Displacement

Wallerstein/Hilliard

Arban

BB 3.3

Hilliard

The Beggar

Brett

Appoggiatura

(to lean against)

Hilliard

Sinfonia

Pergolesi

La Folia

Hilliard

Kosleck

Hummel

Kurt

Hilliard

L'Arlesienne Intermezzo

Bizet

Getcha

Hilliard

Arpeggio

Hilliard

Una Furtiva Lagrima
from the opera L'Elisir d'Amore

Donizetti

Solfège

Rodophe/Hilliard

Lascia ch'io Pianga

Händel
ed. Hilliard

Boogaloo

Hilliard

Stabat Mater
Aria

Pergolesi
ed. Hilliard

Contraction

Hilliard

Struttin' Large

Hilliard

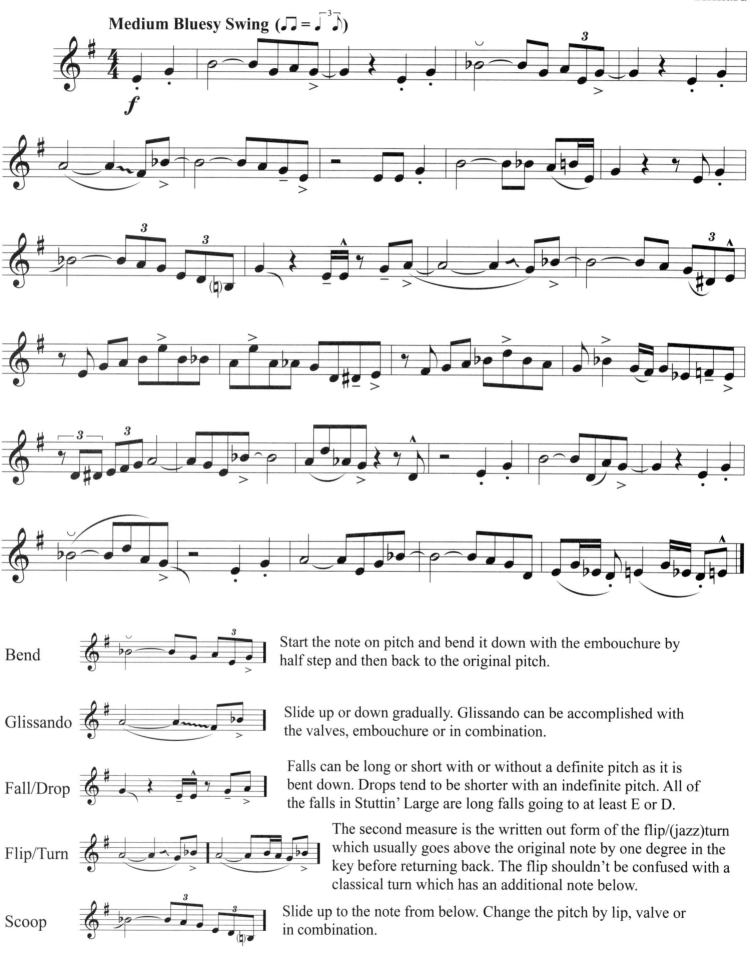

Bend — Start the note on pitch and bend it down with the embouchure by half step and then back to the original pitch.

Glissando — Slide up or down gradually. Glissando can be accomplished with the valves, embouchure or in combination.

Fall/Drop — Falls can be long or short with or without a definite pitch as it is bent down. Drops tend to be shorter with an indefinite pitch. All of the falls in Stuttin' Large are long falls going to at least E or D.

Flip/Turn — The second measure is the written out form of the flip/(jazz)turn which usually goes above the original note by one degree in the key before returning back. The flip shouldn't be confused with a classical turn which has an additional note below.

Scoop — Slide up to the note from below. Change the pitch by lip, valve or in combination.

Schantl

Balquidder Lasses

English 19th c.

Galant Saxon

Hilliard

Concone

March

Hilliard

Themes from Mozart's Opera
Nozze di Figaro

Kling

Vecchetti

Dixieland Rag

Hilliard

Ave Maria

attr. Caccini
arr. Hilliard

Concone

Ländler

Hilliard

Sonata

Mozart

Bordogni
ed. Hilliard

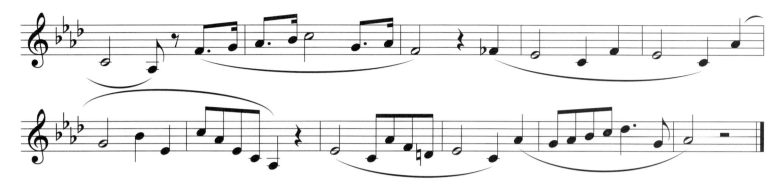

Advice to Cupid

T. Vincent

Hemiola

Hilliard

Bordogni
ed. Hilliard

Hasse

Samba

Seiter

Serenade

Schubert

Accelerated Air Flow

Variations on a Theme by Hummel

Kosleck

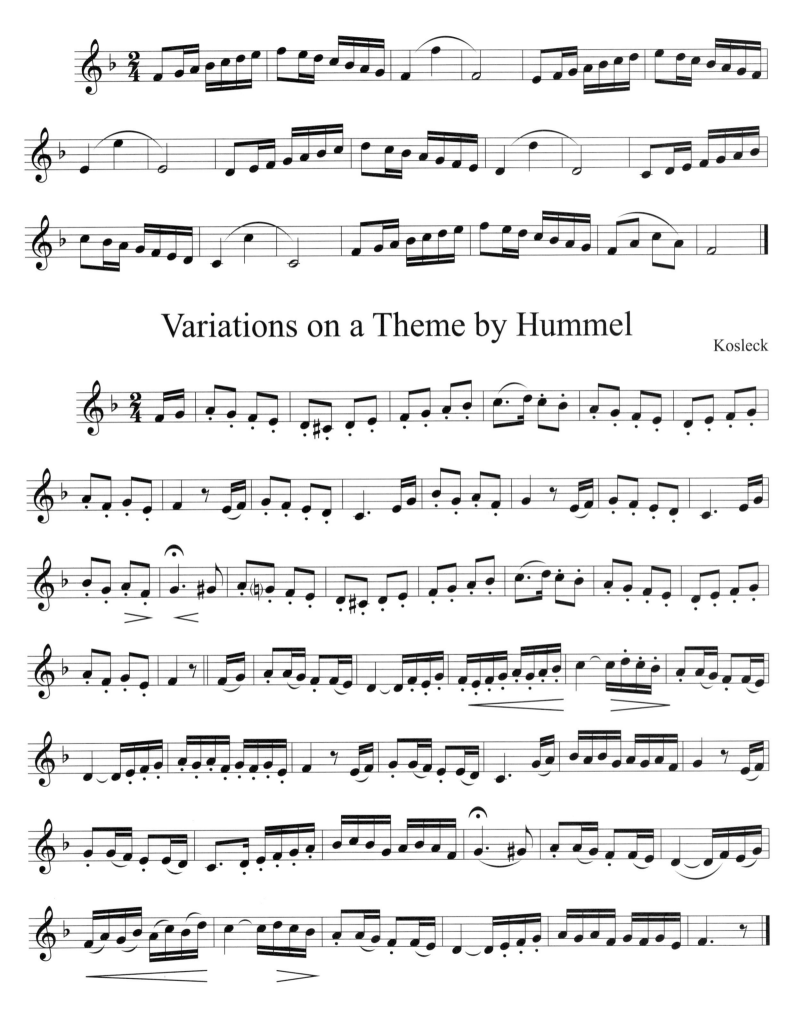

Surrounded

Hilliard

Boppin'

Wermuth

Bluesin' It

Wermuth

Accelerated Air Flow

44

Intermediate Studies Performance Guide

Menuet, French Dance, Dance of the Pharaohs, King of Sweden's March, Water Music and Royal Wedding Dance – Dance forms (including the march) comprise one of the main cornerstones in music. Rhythmic constancy, the feel of the meter and knowing which notes to stress are critical.

Flow Study – The great trumpet teacher Vincent Cichowicz made this pattern famous. This version is a very efficient and developmentally appropriate warm-up for intermediate trumpet players. Memorize it! Buy Cichowicz's complete "Long Tone Studies" from Balquhidder Music. http://www.balquhiddermusic.com/

Direction – The title is about phrase direction and melodic contour. Bar one leads to the down beat of bar two. Each eight bar section should have a distinctly different feel.

Arban – This is essentially a chromatic bugle call. A dry articulation with lots of bite on the front end.

Hooked by Degree – The hooked steps should flow forward; even at a slow tempo.

Kling – This is a very soulful etude. Be careful of transitions between triplet and dotted rhythms.

Jig – The jig is one of the most popular folk dance forms with its origin in Ireland. The BBC World Service has used *Lilliburlero*, a similar jig from the 17th century as its signature sign-on tune for decades.

Minuet – In most minuets one and three are stressed. In this minuet three is slightly less important than one.

Chromatic – Lead to the dotted quarter. Practice the fingerings by themselves as needed.

Arban – Use a hard articulation that rebounds quickly on the accents.

Pie Jesu – A simple but sensuous aria for soprano in the Catholic tradition. Listen to a good recording of one of the greatest sacred works composed that casts a spell on the listener.

Rudolf – Have fun with this very playful etude.

Aida Triumphal March – This is the actual trumpet part lifted directly from the opera score. Play it in a grandiose manner.

Exuberance – This etude mimics the Swing style from the big band era. Play this in a hard swing that is somewhere in the middle between ♫=♪♪ and ♫=♪♪ swung eighth note ratio.

Gavotta – Enjoy one of Corelli's best themes.

Hilliard Allegretto – Make a big stylistic contrast between the staccato and legato themes.

Lip Slur – These lip slurs are an easy preparatory flexibility exercise for the next etude "Mambo Slurs."

Mambo Slurs – Most Latin music is played with straight eighths and emphasizes the syncopated notes. This etude falls in the broad category of Mambo. Use it to dance your way to better slurs.

Displacement – Use this popular dance melody by Wallerstein to explore how a melody changes character when it is set on a different beat.

Arban – In the same style as the other Arban.

BB 3.3 – Listen to the Brandenburg Concerto #3, third movement, to mimic the Baroque string style with a heavy accent on one.

The Beggar – Use this tune to practice your dotted eighth rhythms. Keep it snappy!

Appoggiatura – The appoggiatura is the key to Western music in a nutshell. Dissonance vs. Consonance, Tension vs. Release. The grace note appoggiaturas are played as two even notes with the grace note on the beat. The first note is stressed and usually lands on a strong pulse.

Pergolesi Sinfonia – A masterpiece from the proto-Classical period and a great opportunity to practice the appoggiatura. Listen to a recording for the style of this genius who died at twenty-six.

La Folia – A Portuguese peasant dance melody that dates back to the Renaissance.

Kosleck Turns – Turns look scary, but they're not hard. Follow the shape of the turn sign. Go up then down. The accidentals below the sign affect the lowest note of the turn. Accidentals above affect the highest note of the turn. Begin slow and make sure you start them in time on the second eighth note of beat two.

Hummel – Try the turn as sixteenths and thirty-seconds to see which one feels right.

Kurt – Observe the variety of articulations.

L'Arlesienne Intermezzo – This solo has been lifted directly from the horn part of the L'Arlesienne Second Suite. It's not well known because the horn is buried an octave below the saxophone part. Only use the breath marks indicated if you have to break the phrase.

Getcha – Gotcha Getchell!

Arpeggio – A painless way to practice arpeggios in a small range.

Una Furtiva Lagrima – This is the bassoon solo at the beginning of the aria. The *calando* is exaggerated.

Rodolphe – Listen for the written out appoggiaturi in this Solfège.

Lascia ch'io Pianga – This aria was often sung by *castrati* in Händel's day. Listen to the florid baroque ornamentation on this piece in the movie *Farinelli*. This alternate *da capo* version is much simpler.

Boogaloo – In the 1960s, Boogaloo became a very popular jazz style fusing R&B and Soul with Cuban Mambo and Son Montuno. Puerto Rican musicians who played this fusion coined the term Boogaloo.

Stabat Mater – The long appoggiaturi followed by the valve trill are very unusual – exaggerate them. This piece is very dramatic. Find a recording to listen to that captures the drama.

Contraction – Quarters are long and heavy. Bounce the eighth notes and let them flow.

Struttin' Large – A bluesy swing with a coarse swagger. Included, is a glossary of five jazz ornaments used in the etude. The falls should be long, descending to either E or D depending on your preference.

Schantl Largo – From the third volume of Viennese horn player Anton Schantl's four volumes. Highly idiomatic.

Balquidder Lasses – The earliest printed version of this tune is in 4/4 time. It's often done in cut time. Try it both ways.

Galant Saxon – This etude was inspired by the Saxon Hasse. He wrote in the Galant style which coincided with the late Baroque period but also shares elements of the emerging Classical style. Play this piece with an effortless elegance that makes it sing.

Concone – Like all of the Concone, this is a vocalise. A vocalise is a vocal exercise sung without words that usually has a piano accompaniment. Make it sing.

March – Contemporary march with a major/minor twist.

Kling Mozart – Kling strings together lots of melodies from "Nozze di Figaro." He wasn't the first to do this, but this is a great arrangement.

Vecchietti – Unknown but incredibly gifted melodist and horn player who taught brass at the *Accademia di Santa Cecilia* in Rome when it became a secular organization in the 1870s.

Dixieland Rag – The rag is one of the oldest Dixieland forms going back to the late 1800s. Dixieland in general and rags in particular are done very fast and with straight eighths, but can take on a light swing at slower tempos making it feel more like the music that succeeded it of the Swing era.

Ave Maria – Composed by Vladimir Vavilov around 1970, it is a musical hoax generally misattributed to Baroque composer Giulio Caccini.

Concone – The first measure of the fourth line has a common vocal "sob" used in opera.

Ländler – A German peasant dance. Most of the down beat slurs should have extra weight on them when they act as a written out appoggiatura. Play it with gusto and be one of the *volk*.

Mozart Sonata – Piano Sonata #16. Let the sixteenths spin forward with pianistic ease and an operatic line.

Bordogni – The Bordogni vocalises are almost identical in style to Concone.

Advice to Cupid – English composer Thomas Vincent caught in the shadow of his contemporary Händel.

Hemiola – A hemiola creates the impression of a meter change (i.e., measure eight).

Bordogni – Vocalise

Hasse – This exercise is very similar to some Kopprasch exercises but a slightly better grade of music.

Samba – An emblematic form used during Carnival in Rio De Janeiro, Brazilian samba has become an icon of the national identity. Chris Seiter's happy and festive *Samba* offers lots of syncopated rhythms. Start by counting the piece in 4/4. Then, when the rhythms are mastered, move to cut time for the full effect. Slurs terminating on an articulation are connected but tongued.

Schubert Serenade – An "art song" so popular it became part of the *parlour* repertory. Don't hold the sugar.

Accelerated Air Flow – Use the same accelerated air on the sixteenths as you do on the octave slur. These patterns cover modal scales (important for jazz, early music pre-1750, post romantic composers Debussy and Bartók, and folk music) that are often neglected by band programs.

Hummel Variations – Use the Accelerated Air Flow exercise to get ready for the fast sixteenths in the Hummel variation.

Surrounded – This exercise targets the concept of approaching chord notes with surround tones in a medium swing. Surround tones and stepwise and chromatic approach tones are essential and fundamental elements of the "bebop" jazz improv language emphasized in Bruce Wermuth's etudes.

Boppin' – When performing this piece, strive for fluidity and full lengths on the eighth note lines unless otherwise indicated. In a jazz swing piece with extended pairs of slurred eighth notes, phrases often start on accented upbeat eighths and continue with accents on eighth note offbeats. This type of offbeat eighth note accenting, while maintaining fluidity with coupled slurs (or coupling with legato tonguing), is a defining feature of jazz bebop performance. There are three flip/turns in this exercise. Refer to the examples on p.26 for explanation.

Bluesin' It – The chromatic surrounding and embellishing tones are used to approach and connect chord tones on the strong beats within the melody of this standard blues harmonic progression. Melodic embellishment of this kind, forms a central component of the bebop genre, in both written and improvised melodies. As in *Boppin'*, strive for fluidity and sustain the eighth notes unless it's the last eighth note of the phrase with a staccato.

About the Author

Howard Hilliard is a fifth generation Californian where he studied at the University of Southern California and received his Bachelor and Master of Music. At the invitation of principal conductor Zubin Mehta, he was invited to play principal horn in L'Orchestra del Maggio Musicale Fiorentino (Florence Italy's main orchestra) for over six years. As part of that orchestra he recorded on many of the major classical labels as well as the original "Three Tenors" concert from Rome, which was the biggest selling classical CD of all time. After returning to the United States, Dr. Hilliard received his doctoral degree from the University of North Texas College of Music. His most recent concerto engagements in Texas include multiple performances with the Garland, Las Colinas, San Angelo and Symphony Arlington orchestras.

Dr. Hilliard has performed as principal horn in numerous symphonies through out the United States, Europe and Latin America. Orchestras and wind ensembles he has performed as principal horn with include: "I Solisti Fiorentini", "Solisti dell'Ensemble Cameristico Pistoiese", "Orquesta Sinfónica de la UANL" in Monterrey, Mexico, Boston Civic Symphony, North Shore Symphony, Dallas Chamber Orchestra, Plano Symphony, East Texas Symphony, Waco Symphony Orchestra, Irving Symphony, Dallas and Texas Wind Symphonies, Corpus Christi Symphony, Riverside County Philharmonic, West Side Symphony, Burbank Chamber Orchestra, Glendale Chamber Orchestra, American Youth Symphony, and Desert Symphony. He is currently the principal horn of the Garland, Las Colinas, San Angelo, Dallas Pops and Symphony Arlington orchestras.

Some of the conductors Dr. Hilliard has played principal horn for include: Riccardo Muti, Carlo Maria Guilini, Eduardo Mata, Andrew Davis, Leonard Slatkin, Georges Prètre, Esa-Pekka Salonen, Christian Thielemann, Myung-Wha Chung, Semyon Bychkov, James Conlon, Frederick Fennell as well as Zubin Mehta. He has been a voting member of the National Academy of Recording Arts and Science, which selects the "Grammy" awards each year. In addition to being an active freelancer in the DFW Metroplex, he teaches French horn and trumpet, repairs brass instruments, does custom horn work and publishes both pedagogical articles and sheet music. His publication "Lip Slurs for Horn" is the best-selling book of lip slurs for horn in the world. Sold through Hal Leonard on six continents and used by members of major symphony orchestras throughout the world as well as beginning horn classes throughout Texas, it was featured in clinics at the 2012 International Horn Symposium. Dr. Hilliard's articles have been published in his field's most prestigious journals of record including; *The Horn Call, The International-al Trumpet Guild Journal, The Instrumentalist* and TMEA *Bandmasters Review.*